The Poor ShoeMaker

KENNETH DAVID BRUBACHER

The Poor Shoemaker

AuthorHouse™
1663 Liberty Drive
Bloomington, IN 47403
www.authorhouse.com
Phone: 1 (800) 839-8640

A Hat & Hammer Production
A Division of Brubacher Technologies Ltd.
Visit: hat&hammerproductions.com

Made in Canada

Published by AuthorHouse 11/23/2015

ISBN: 978-1-5049-5365-8 (sc)
ISBN: 978-1-5049-5367-2 (hc)
ISBN: 978-1-5049-5366-5 (e)

Library of Congress Control Number: 2015916213

Print information available on the last page.

This book is printed on acid-free paper.

Art by

Taffese Lemma

Addis Ababa   Ethiopia

Special thanks to

Tezera Ketema

Without whose patient assistance this wonderful art

Could not have graced these pages

This book is for

Donna

Whose forbearance of the author's foibles
Is doubtless already legendary

nce upon

A long time ago
There was a shoemaker
He was poor
Shoemakers are always poor in stories
They are also poor in real life
Right now

he poor shoemaker

Lived with his wife in a very small house

It was also his shoemaking shop

They had two children   A girl and a boy

They did not help

With the making of shoes

In point of fact

They did not do very much of anything at all

he shoemaker was poor

Not because he made bad shoes
He made very good shoes
People paid him a fair price for the shoes
He was poor because he took pity on other people
Who had hardly anything at all
Some were sick and could not work
Some were hungry and had no real home

hen the shoemaker

Was paid for the shoes and had some coins
He took pity on the poor people in the street
And gave them many of his coins
He kept enough coins for his family
But he ended up with not very many
Extra coins for fancy things

his drove his wife nuts

She would yell at him
You make some good money
And then give it all away
Here I have barely enough coins to buy food
Much less a new dress
Never in my life have I seen such a loser
Then she would stomp off in a huff

Lots of people do this   Stomp off in a huff

I have never seen a huff   But huffs must be plenty big

After all   People always get into them

Or they could not stomp off in one

Also a huff must be open at the bottom

Or the people stomping off in them

Could not get their feet on the ground to do their

Stomping Off

One day the King came by

He came with a whole bunch of his people

Who did things for Kings

When the King went out to do stuff

The King had been hunting in a nearby forest

Where one of the hunting dogs

Had ripped off the Kings boot

And was busy eating it

ipping off the King's boot

Or anything else attached to a King
Is Not A Good Thing To Do
And if you then eat this thing
That is ripped off the King
It is a Very Very Bad Thing Indeed To Do
Pretty sure that the dog who ate the boot
Soon found out about this

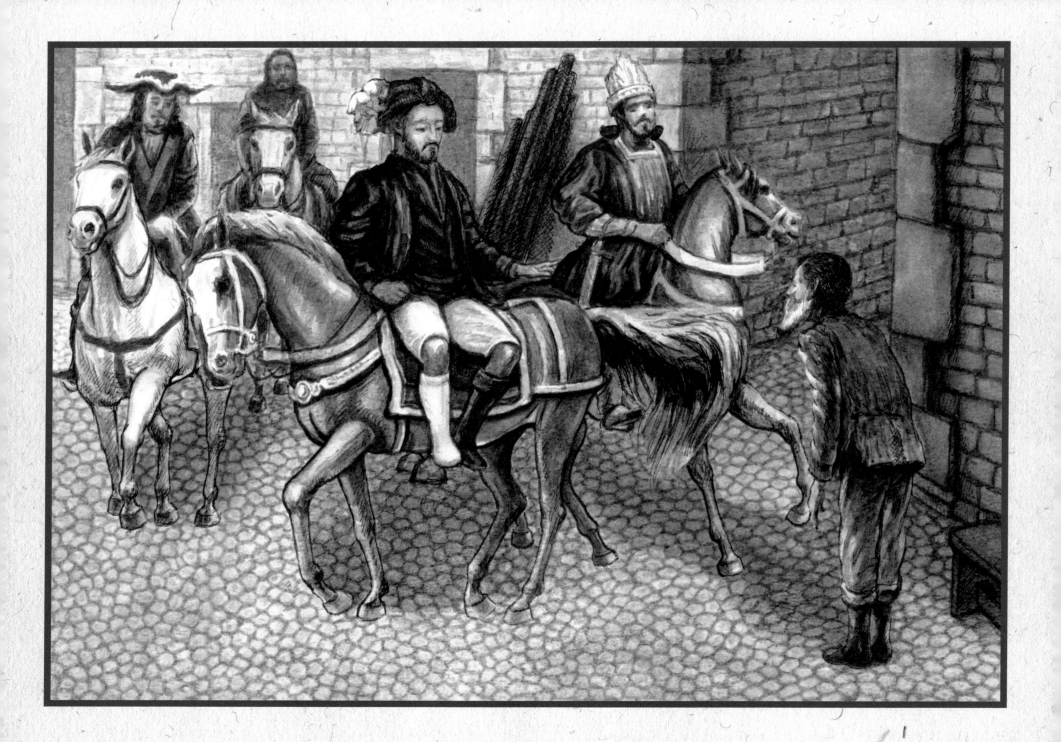

o the King had only one boot

And was not happy
Also   if the King was not happy
His people had good reason to be unhappy too
And his people would try anything to fix it
They asked Where is a shoemaker
This is how the king came to our poor shoemaker

he King

Rode up to the house of the poor shoemaker

One of his helpers took the poor shoemaker out

To meet the King and his one boot

The King told the shoemaker to make new boots for him

The shoemaker bowed down to the King

Until his head was right down touching the street

And said that he would be very pleased to do this

he King said OK

But what boots to wear while going to lunch
The shoemaker who was very clever
He said that the King
Would wear the shoemakers own boots
Until the King came back from lunch
So the King and his people went off for lunch

ut now

The shoemaker had a problem

All his elves were off work

On sick leave or holidays   or W.S.B

On account of whacking thumbs with hammers

Or such

So the shoemaker was high and dry

owever

Our shoemaker was clever

Very much indeed he was clever

He had seen something

That other shoemakers had not seen

This was that both his feet were not the same

The right and left feet were different

p until that time

Shoes were made the same for both feet
You simply pulled them on and it did not matter
Which one went onto which foot
But our clever shoemaker had seen that
Feet are different
He decided that this time
He would make shoes to fit each foot properly

Our poor

But clever shoemaker

Had kept a pattern of his own boots

He knew that they fitted the King

So the shoemaker quickly revised the patterns

In the new way

And made boots for the King

he King came back from his lunch

Where are my boots

The shoemaker brought them out to the King

They were fitted onto the King

What are these boots that fit my feet   said the King

The shoemaker told the King what he had done

The King was very happy

The King thanked the shoemaker

For his new and better boots

He said that he would show them to rich people

He also promised that the shoemaker

Would become very wealthy because of

His Better Shoe Idea

The shoemaker bowed low to the ground

As the King threw him a bag of coins

There were quite a few coins in the bag

The shoemaker was very happy with them
But almost before he had counted all the coins
The tax collector came
And took away about half of his coins
His name was Zackariah Elijah Uss   Mister Zack E Uss
The shoemaker did not like this
But what could he do

e gave coins to the people

Who brought him wood for his fireplace
And the food for his family
Then he gave coins to the people in the street
People who had no money or a place to stay
He also gave coins to the mothers
With hungry children and they could not feed them
And to those who could not walk

Then his wife came back home

She had heard about the King and the bag of coins
But soon learned that nearly all the coins were gone
The shoemaker had kept back enough to live OK
But his wife wanted money to buy fancy things
She yelled at him for being a loser
Then went out back to fetch her huff
And stomped out again

The shoemaker

Took all this in silence
He never answered back to his wife
And went on quietly making shoes
Then he waited   And waited some more
He had faith in the King and his kind words
About reward for his Great Idea

He waited   and waited   but the King never came

He had sold his Idea to a fellow named Gucci

This is a lesson   Do not put faith in the promises of Kings

Invest in companies like Gucci

It is also a lesson in that the real world does not work

Like Robin Hood and his henchbuddies

The real world works by oppressing the poor

While the rich get richer

The shoemakers wife tripped over her huff

Banged her head on the stones and died

His daughter ran off with a convict

His son sold vacuum cleaners This perhaps a good job

But electricity was a few centuries yet off

So business was slow

The shoemaker was now all alone

He gave coins to the poor people on the street

He learned to make baked beans

And chicken noodle soup from Dead Scratch

It was never known how he got to meet Mister Scratch

Now deceased   Or from where he came

The soup and beans were very good

A man can eat well on bread and butter

And cheese and soup and baked beans

For a long time

When he was very old and died

He had no money in the bank down the street
Yet there were a lot of people   Mostly poor
Who followed the wagon with the body of the
Shoemaker in the Box
They followed the wagon to the place where they buried him
You see He was poor in coin But yet a very rich man
in Friends and good deeds in helping many other people

 am more than sure that

Today he Lives in a place

Where he has many friends

And where there is much coin laid up for him

In a

Bank of a Different Nature

ABOUT THE AUTHOR

Kenneth David Brubacher was born into a large family of sort of Mennonites in Elmira, through no fault of his own. He was encouraged to make an attempt at becoming a normal human being, but with limited success. To the surprise of nearly everyone he graduated from secondary school in 1970.

From there he traveled the world extensively turning his hand to many kinds of jobs and eventually returned to Elmira having accomplished very little. He got work as a millwright but it soon was clearly evident that he was a millwrong. After being mercifully fired from that job he went trucking and almost immediately distinguished himself summa cum laude (with oak leaf cluster and Silver Star) by destroying the truck.

He got married and begat two lovely daughters which took after their mother in many wonderful ways and turned out normal. It was considered a blessing that he had no sons because there was a high degree of probability that if he had sons the little morons would turn out like their dad.

Knowing little about shoes and even less about feet he then took over his father's shop and started to make shoes by hand on April Fools' Day 1978. Very few people caught on. It was obvious that people whose feet were so bad they sought out the services of a cobbler were not very fussy. The business prospered in spite of its inherent inadequacies.

He also applied himself to many varieties of sport, establishing a universal mediocrity in their pursuit seldom seen. When his body was sufficiently trashed he took up umpiring baseball where it was observed that his training must have occurred under the tender administrations of the CNIB.

Currently he makes his home on a rented farm near Creemore and repairs a few shoes in his small shop in Collingwood. The farmhouse will soon become a gravel pit whereupon it was his intent to establish institutions where Mennonites could go to seek quiet enjoyment. This, of course, until it was pointed out to him that somebody had already done it. These establishments are known as Mennonite Farms.

The author heartily recommends that any reader who takes a notion to write and produce a book or a play, to lie down on the couch and play videos of fawns gamboling in a sun-splashed meadow full of butterflies - until the feeling goes away.

It is hoped that you enjoy the book and that its contents and presentation may provide therapeutic assistance in the remedy of your insomnia.

Printed in the United States
By Bookmasters